Where the Sanity Ends

Where the Sanity Ends

Poems, rants, and tirades by
Michelle Lang
Drawings, scribbles, and doodles by
Holli Jacobson

Special Friendship Edition

RBL*Publishing*

WHERE THE SANITY ENDS

Published by RBL PUBLISHING 2019
© 2019 RBL STUDIOS

For permissions contact:
Assist@RelaxationBasedLifestyle.com

ISBN: 978-1-7322636-2-8
HARDBACK: 978-1-7322636-5-9
E-Book ISBN: 978-1-7322636-6-6

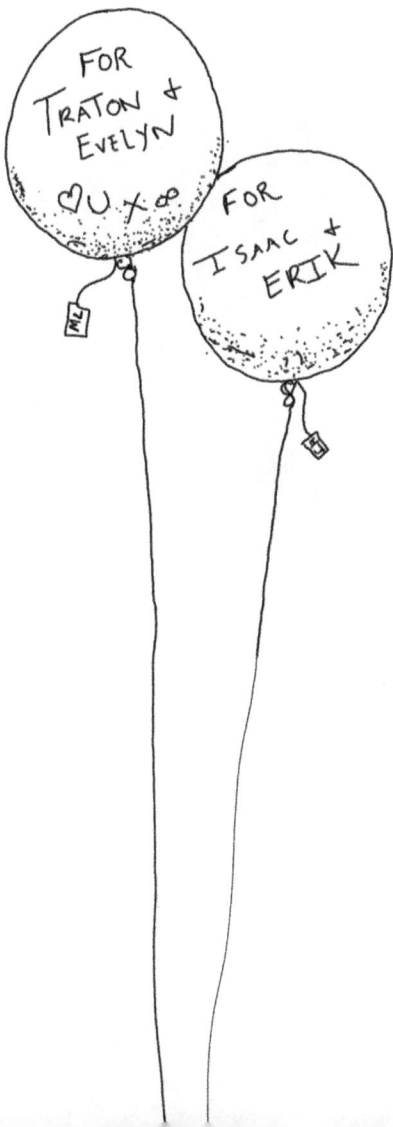

Where the Sanity Ends

INVITATION

If you're a drowsy-er, come in,
If you're a drowsy-er, a wisher you could
get sleep more-er, a
Hope-er, a pray-er that your nap will
happen sometime today-er...
If you're a pretender dressed in a cape
made of tape and erase-er...come in!
For we have some bonding tales to spin...
Come in!
Come in!

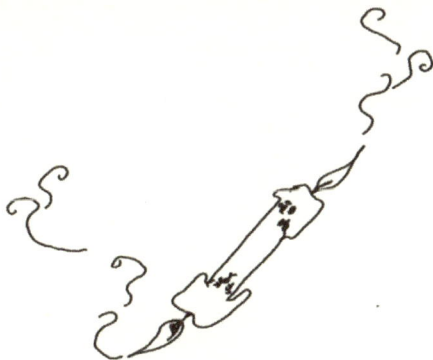

PAINTING

Wow. Your painting is so stunning!
Is that a little man running?
And see this cool negative shape?
I like how the colors
are blending.
And the spiral here --
has so much energy, such intensity.
I mean, this line is so tall!!!
I just love it all...
if only it weren't on the wall.

BIRTHDAY SURPRISE

I baked cupcakes to bring to my son's
preschool for his birthday soiree.
I made them myself and
I'm excited to see
just how happy
all the kids will be
with the fluorescent blue frosting
and the green monster eyes.
(Cake Boss would be proud, I do surmise.)
So, I get there,
and this kid jeers at me,
"Excuse me, are those gluten free?"
Another one snorts with disdain,
"And are they made with honey?"
And a third juts out her chest,
"Those don't look store bought...
you know, with money."
The barage just keeps coming.
"Is there artificial flavoring in there?"
"Did you pin back your hair?"
"Did you wear gloves and a mask?"
And then one little one pees
all down her knees.
And that's when I take off
RUNNING.

A THOUGHT TO MY BABY

If I told the TSA agent
My cold brew
was for you...
do you think they would let
me through?

MY SHOPPING LIST

"Alexa, add bread, lemons, and
cottonelle to *My List*."
How handy! I love this.
So, now, when I go to the store
I don't have to carry around a
pesky sheet of paper anymore!

Alexa, what's on my list?

Poop
Gummy bears
Stinky feet
Poop
Ghostbusters
Poop poop poop poop
Butt
Poop
Bread
Parmesan
Tacos
Poop
Poop
Poop
Poop to your mom
Poop

Poop
Poop
Poop
Poop
Poop
Mashed potatoes poop green poop
Poop
Poop

It's really handy. Thank you, Alexa.
I was wondering what to buy.
I sure hope the store has a massive poop supply.

BAD HOUSE GUEST

You drink all my OJ.
And you never offer to buy more.
And you throw your towels
all bunched up
on the floor.
You buy a ton of stuff
and make me keep it all.
You ignore the
"Shoes off at the door" sign
hanging in the hall.
You never hang up your coat
or do your own laundry.
(Even though I've told you it's YOUR
responsibility.)
You leave dishes on the table.
And you don't help with a single chore.
But I'll cut you some slack
because you're only four.

THE INSTAGRAM TRIP

The photos from our family trip
are such a delight.

(I didn't post the one of you puking
all over me
during the flight.
Or the epic three hour meltdown
"someone" had on the train.
And I left out all that excruciating
diarrheal pain.)

Everyone is smiling and looking so good!
ALL OF THE TIME.
Just like they should.

BABYSITTER

Thank you for coming,
that all went pretty great.
You were only 35 minutes late!
And you broke my kid's shelf,
and left dishes in the sink,
and wait, on the curtains there, is that,
what is THAT... *INK*?
And what is that?
Pee pee, behind my chair?
You provide what kind of care?
And my office papers are strewn everywhere.
You put them to bed,
and turned on the TV...
when midnight rolled around
you sent a text to me,
"I'm done watching fuller house.
Can you come home?"
What?
Getting paid 18 dollars an hour
isn't enough
to sit around all alone?
You're fired!
You're out!
Never again!
Say, are you available next Saturday?
Great, see you then.

DROP OFF

Oh, drop off,
how I despise you.
First the waking,
and then the yelling,
and then the pee pee diaper smelling.
The dress rejection,
egg demanding,
waffle toasting,
cereal pouring,
tummy ache moaning,
duce dropping,
EPIC
shoe battle.
The car squabbling.
Now the carsickness complaining.
And the,"who farted?!?" exclaiming.
And the drop-off.
You hold my leg,
And look so sad.
I play with you and
think you're okay.
But as I'm just about out the door,
you burst into sobs,
and fall on the floor.
I wonder if you'll have a good day.
And as I drive away,
you start to play.
I breathe a deep sigh of relief.

DEAR MOM

I saved all my cries for you.
I've been holding them in all day.
Out in the yard where I was trying to play.
The teacher said, "No!"
"Don't do that."
and
"Be nice."
I told them I got hit first,
but no one cared.
I sucked in my pride,
not letting the hurt show from the inside.
But now that you're here
the clenching of my feelings
comes flooding out to the ceiling.
I scream and yell.
You ask me, "When will it stop?"
But I just cannot tell.
I feel safe with you
to let it all out.
It's not relaxing, I know,
but it's how I show
I love you.

KID to PARENT day

I get to DRIVE?!?
And do dishes in the SINK!?!?
And you're not going to tell me how much
juice to DRINK?
I get to watch TV?
As long as I want?
And pay the bills?
Sure, I'll rip them up.
What's that you say?
It's my turn
to clean the toilet bowl?!?
Pour the twisty blue gel down the gaping
hole?
Dinner needs COOKING?
And it's up to me?
YIPPPPPPPIE!
I love being you SO MUCH!

PARENT to KID day

I get to take a NAP?
And someone is going to pack my lunch?
I get to lay around all day
and have MORE snacks to munch?
You mean
those goldfish
won't go right to my thigh?
And I get to be the one to poke
YOU in the eye?
Hold on…hold up.
Someone is coming to teach me Spanish?
And they will help me paint?
And I get to eat all that ice cream
without taking lactate?
What's that you say?
You DON'T want my help?
I don't have to wash a single dish?
THAT'S your wish?
You want me to get out of your way?
To go read in my room
all alone?

This day is the best!
I love being you SO MUCH!

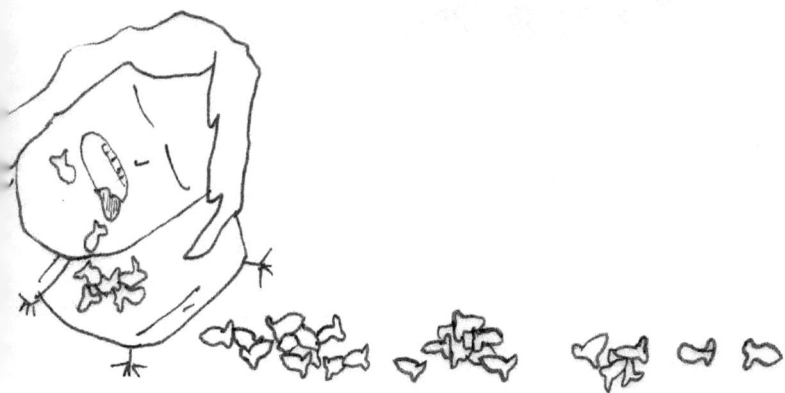

THE GIVER

No more fundraisers!
I'm not giving any more!
I just gave thirty bucks
to a drum circle
I don't want to attend.
And I purchased three hundred dollars
of coupons
I won't even spend!
Now I got an envelope
wanting me to put in a donation
for an eatery somewhere in town...
and you want me to go get pledges
for the jog-a-thon crown?
You pass me a flyer that says,
"Don't forget to buy a CD!"
Hold on.
Those discs were donated by ME!
I don't want it! I don't! I want to go home.
Fine, here's another fifty bucks.
Now just let me alone.

DETOX

I'm doing a detox.
So I can feel better,
all healthy and pure.
Got my lemons.
And red pepper flakes.
But not eating all day has given me the
shakes.
I'll make a smoothie to tide me over.
If I put chocolate chips in my smoothie...
it still counts as a detox, I think.
(I mean, it's not like I'm having
wine to drink.)
Besides, they say coco is good for you,
so that's what I'll do.
And then...
just...
a...................................... ....

.   . . .handful of popcorn.
Some cookies,
nachos,
cheeze-its and lunch meat.
There.
Detox complete.

Wait...did I cheat?

VACATION

I don't want to be stressy,
or seem full of hate,
but I mean, you GUYS,
we're running 45 minutes late!!!
And everyone's crying.
And no one wants to go pee.
"PUT YOUR SHOES ON!"
Why is no one listening to me?
Last night I packed the cooler,
and all the snacks,
while you kids and your father
got to relax.
I've been prepping the car,
buying the tickets to the zoo,
and all I ask is you put on your damn shoe!
Just put on the shoe!
And get in the car!
I really need some coffee,
but that's probably going too far.
No one says thank you
or even recognizes
that this vacation is more work
than most exercises.
We're going! We're on the road.
We'll get there by three!
What's that?
Pullover.
NOW you have to pee?!?

WORKING MOM

It's not hard to write poems
when you're really quite sad,
and half the food in the
refrigerator is bad.
Because I haven't been home
the last couple of nights.
But don't worry
I'm sure the kids lived off of
cheetos,
cookies,
and candy coated ice cream--
It's not a habit, I mean...
I'm sure they'll grow out of it
by the time they're eighteen.
I can't micromanage
and make all the money
and do the birthday cards
and shit rainbows all sunny.
Now the kids are in bed,
and I flip through my phone
I miss them,
as I sit here all alone.
They are only small once
I don't want it to pass me by...
They're so peaceful
when they are sleeping.

DAILY ACTIVITY

My house is a mess.
My eyes need a rest.
Is that a lump in my breast?!?
Nope. Thank God.
Just a chunk of Rice-Krispy Treat.
Oh, good.
I wanted something to eat.

HEADACHE

Do you have a headache?
I'll fix it Mommy!
I have a song that will make
you want to play with me.
I'll bang on this pan.
And sing at the top of my lungs.
Then strobe the lights,
isn't this fun?
Are you feeling better yet?
What's that you say?
You can't take anymore noise?
You're ready to go outside and play?
Sounds good, mommy.
Let's bring the bull horn,
what do you say?

SUNSET

This day has been confiscated.
I feel so frustrated.
The shit is hitting the fan.
Nothing's going according to plan.
It's got to be five or six...
what dinner I should fix?
No? Wait.
That can't be right.
Nine-thirty?
In the morning?
I remember the days when I used to sleep
until then.
But not anymore!
I've already been to the store.
And the park.
And cleaned TWO rounds of oatmeal
off the floor.
It's like having three days in one!
I'm getting so much done.
And yet the days are so....
unproductive.

CIRCLE OF LIFE

I help you with you.
I help you with us.
You help us with us.
But who helps me?
Oh, I get it.

No-bo-dy.

PARMESAN CHEESE

Oh, Doodlie-Doodlie
I'm down on my knees
picking you out of the
floorboards.
I wish there was a way
to ban you today
But, alas, there isn't.

RE-USEABLE DIAPERS

They save the environment
and they come in such cute colors,
plus, they don't irritate the skin.
All of this is a huge mommy win!
You can buy them in bulk
and they pack up so nice.
Your friends will think
you're so crunchy and wise!
Just ignore the poop
leaking out the back,
and the puddle of wet
seeping into your lap.
Don't worry that your car seats
hold the musky scent of urine...
and the bedding needs changing
and so does the rug.

Man, re-useable diapers sure do amaze.
They are handy and great.
They make you feel earthy and green!
You'll love them.
I promise.
So long as you like to spend your days
trying not to SCREAM!

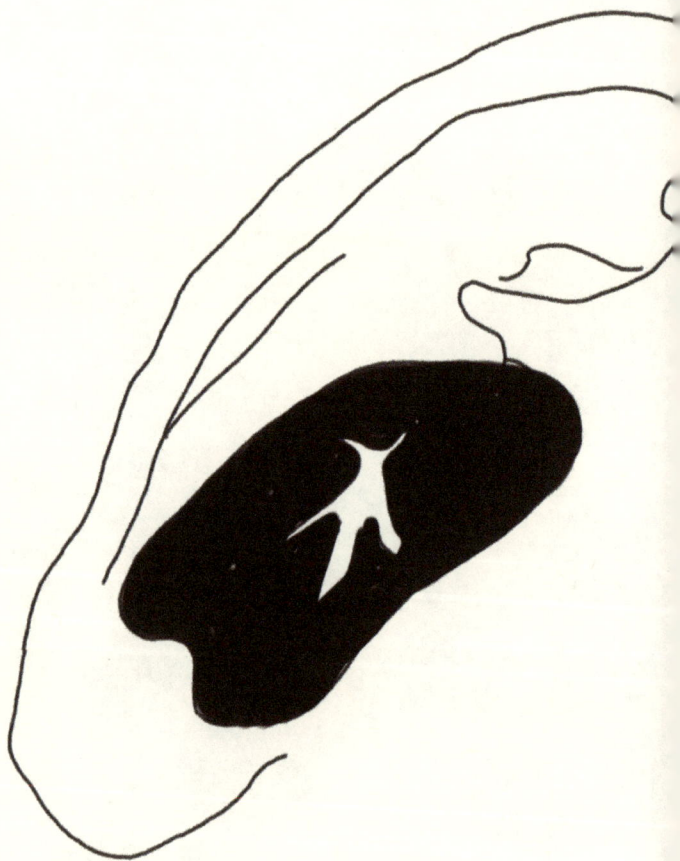

DARK DAY

I'm sure I'm ugly to you.
I'm stressed and angry,
mentally I'm through.
I'm done, I've had it
and yet I can't call it quits.
I'm the one running the bloody ship!
I'm overworked
and underpaid
and no, I don't feel like getting laid.
I want a massage
and not the dirty kind.
I want a spa day
to try to unwind.
I need some time to be peaceful inside.
I know all the angst is not pretty
and I fully realize...
YOU'RE tired and run down too.
But you're NOT being debonair.
You don't take me on dates,
you don't ask me for drinks,
there's no movie popcorn,
or soft, playful winks.
So yes, I'm ugly to you.
But you're ugly to me, too.

GOOD MORNING

It's too early to be up.
Get out of here!
Your little foot in my face
and your butt on my gut.
Now you're stepping on me.
Pulling my hair.
And yelling "MOMMMMMMMEEEEEE"
I just got kicked in the head!
FINE.
I'll get out of bed.

BEACH

I'll do it.
No me!
I've got it.
Too much!
Now it's all over...
just let it be.
Organic, Australian
sunscreen sure isn't free.
Sand on the blanket.
Sand in the cheese puffs.
Sand up my crack.
NO! DON'T STAND ON MOMMY'S BACK!
Oooo, that really hurt.
Like two stomping elephants' paws
covered in dirt.
Just...give me my shirt.
Forget it.
I'll just sit here.
On my sandy beach towel.
Boy, this is fun.

Can't you tell by my scowl?

MALL

Why are you stopping?
What do you see?
You already have a toy truck
and a fake stuffed puppy.
Put the sucker back. I'm not getting that.
I'm not buying that stupid gnome.
You already have one at home!
No treats, I don't care that it's pink.
Put it back, please.
And I'm not getting those train tracks.
Or the fake rubber snake.
Let's just sit over there and have some snacks.
You just broke it!

ARGH.
Give it to me.
We have to buy it.

KID: "YIPPPPPPPPPPPPIEEEEEE!"

HELLO, GROWN-UP. IT'S ME, DOWN HERE.

Hello! I can hear you.
I'm standing right here.
So when you say
I'm stubborn and hard
and I don't sleep that great
and that I make you stay up too late.
And when you complain
that I make you insane
I can hear you.

AFTER WORK

I yelled at Lou.
Then my husband came
home and yelled at me.
And there we sat, all three,
feeling sad.

MASCARA

I can't find my mascara.
Sure my little one took it.
Probably hid it with her tiara.
Or lost it under her bed.
Or shoved it high inside
that stuffed toy's fluffy head.
Where is my mascara?
I'm going batshit crazy!
Maybe it's with her shoes,
or in the utensils,
or under Daddy's tools...
Maybe near the colored pencils?
Where
is
my
MASCARA!?!

Oh, here it is.
Right where it should be.

THREE BABIES

My husband is sick,
so I have two toddlers to take care of
and ONE BIG BABY.

HOMECOMING PARTY

Spent a week out of town,
and came back to find a week worth of chores
piled up outside my bedroom door.
Bed linens.
Homework.
And a slime of some kind
that has imbedded
itself into the wedding quilt of mine.
The laundry has been "done."
(Which means it's been put in to run.)
This homeccoming party needs less toil
and a little more fun.

DENTIST

When your dental hygienist asks if you're happy
with the color of your teeth
your answer should NOT be:
Oh yes, I like them the same color as pee.
I love my coffee stains
and my broken sealants...
that cavity there?
I don't even feel it!
My bleeding gums
make me feel so alive...
This, **this** is how I
THRIVE.

Wait? What did you say?
My gum line is starting to go away?
What should we do!?!?
Should we patch them?
Or drill them?
Or make them all new?
Whatever it takes.
Let me down easy doc
for goodness-sakes...

Oh, really? No biggie?
Just buy Sensodyne?

But you think I need X-rays?
Nah, I'll get them some other time.

IPAD

Oh, how you frustrate me.
So loud
and distracting with
all your pings and rings
and games
and things.
You never have enough space
to load on a the Lion Kings.
Because you're old
and lame.
NO, NO, NO! Someone help!

Is there a TECHIE on the plane?

You're dying.
You're dead.
Well, kids, for the next four hours
we'll stare at the back of seat 37's head.

THE ONE I CAN'T LIVE WITHOUT

All day.
All night.
You work so hard.
Diapers.
Tissues.
Fabric, by the yard.
You toss 'em.
And grind 'em.
Never stopping to complain.
Even when
your drain
is clogged
with dead skin remains.
And now you're broken.
Oh, washing machine.
What to do
with this pile of clothes
I was going to feed into you?

BRUSHING TEETH

You call it crying.
I say you're opening your mouth
really WIDE.

MAKE THAT DOLLA

My son has a cavity?
Not one, but three?
What do you mean they are too small to see?
How do I know you're telling the truth?
Where is the proof?
Maybe you're just trying
to make my bills go through the roof.
Show me the picture.
That dot? Right there?
That could be dust
or a smear,
or a broken machine.
Look in his mouth!
It's perfectly clean!
I scrub, and I brush,
and I floss, and I swish
two times a day...
and this is how his teeth choose to re-pay?
I'm not getting them filled.
That's it, I've decided.
They are baby teeth.
They'll fall out anyway.
So, who cares if they start to rot?
I will not.
Fine. We'll fill them. Let's rock it.
Yep, no insurance.
We pay out of pocket.

DOCTOR MOM

My kid is screaming her pee pee is hurting
I'll put her to bed?
And hope she feels better in the morning...

UP A HILL

Up a hill
and behind the rail.
Then over the bench
and through the fence.
Can't we just once
walk on the pavement?
I know it'd be no fun.
But you wouldn't trip when you run!
And there'd be a lot less
stubing of your big toe.
Wouldn't it be nice
to sometimes lay low?
To walk on the sidewalk,
like old fogies do.
Instead of seeing a patch of gravel
and plowing right through?
Forget it, go on.
At least let me tie your shoe.

9-5

I hope you had a nice day.
No, no! I'm not saying it's play.
It must be nice, talking with adults who
don't demand to have their own way.
Hope it's been restful
getting to take a wizz,
and eating a snack
and doing your own biz.
Did you enjoy your Facebook flicking?
Lazily watching the time a 'ticking?
And you got to sit and eat lunch?
In SILENCE and consume?
Instead of shoving pistachios in your mouth like
a human vacuum?
But I get it, your day was stressful.
Your pants have a stain.
And your boss is a pain.
I get it. I do.
But it doesn't make me feel bad for you.

THE UNGODLY HOURS

You're so little.
What's your issue?
Why are you up from three to seven
every morning?
Go to sleep you little monkey,
you're making me insane.
And my husband is being so incredibly lame.
He's so annoying,
just laying there.
Sleeping.
What does he think he's doing?
It's 4 a.m.!!!
Why isn't he moving?
Why doesn't he have breasts?
And smell like motherhood?
I know how to fix this.
I'll bang on the wall!
Because if I can't sleep,
then neither can he!
So we ALL fall into the haze
Of INSANITY.

TASTE BUDS

Pumpkin soup from Trader Joe's?
And you LIKE that spicy tortilla chip?
And the tomato dip?
You want my coffee?
And my chocolate beans?
You dig hearts of palm?
And broccoli?
You want my miso soup?
And my sashimi?
Okay, wait, no.
You can't have my martini!
That's where I draw the line.
Twenty years and one month to go
before you can have a sip of mine.

INJURY

I sprained my ankle recently,
and after a few days
it didn't hurt too badly...
unless I tried to do something crazy.

Like put on a sock.

REGISTRATION

What's your birthday?
Got it.
What age did you sit?
Easy as pie.
What age did you stand?
No problem to me.
What age did you walk?
Yep, next question, please.
What age did you feed yourself?
Okay, sure.
No.
Hold on.
What do you mean?
The day my son could pick up
a single garbanzo bean?
Or when he could lick
a tiny spoon clean?
Or are you asking when he could munch on a
sandwich for his lunch?
Or the date he learned how to cook?
Or to bake?
This question must be a mistake.

CALL FROM GREAT GRANNY

Hi! How are you?
Can you hear me?
Kids are a lot of work, I know.
I was alone with YOUR mother in tow.
So many years ago.
Let me tell you,
it was harder then!
My day's been crazy over here.
I played bridge,
and got a pedicure,
and then I went to the store,
and got a pair of shoes I can't afford.
Enough about me.
How's your husband?
Is he stressed?
I sent him some candy the other day.
Did you get it?
I'm thinking of getting a laptop.
Can you make me a blog?
Also, be sure to email me that one photo
of your kid
holding the frog.
You know the one I mean?

Hello, honey?
You there?
Is that...snoring?
We must have a bad connection.
I'll call you back in the morning.

COMMUNICATION

My husband says I repeat things that are bothering me.
My husband says I repeat things that are bothering me.
My husband says I repeat things that are bothering me.
My husband says I repeat things that are bothering me.
My husband says I repeat things that are bothering me.
My husband says I repeat things that are bothering me.
My husband says I repeat things that are bothering me.
My husband says I repeat things that are bothering me.
My husband says I repeat things that are bothering me.
My husband says I repeat things that are bothering me.
My husband says I repeat things that are bothering me.
My husband says I repeat things that are bothering me.
My husband says I repeat things that are bothering me.
My husband says I repeat things that are bothering me.
My husband says I repeat things that are bothering me.
My husband says I repeat things that are bothering me.

I have no idea what he's talking about.

POOP PIG

Let your kid's doodles come out to play!
Don't hide them away.
The brown smudges
and the pencil rubs
are beautiful.
Much better than that
perfectly formed pig
you kid's art teacher did.
Your child's art doesnt' need fixing.

MOMMIE

Mommie?

> I'm standing right here.

Mommie, Mommie, Mommie.

> I'm right here!

Mommie, Mommie, Mommie, Mommie!

Mommie!
Mommie.
Mommie!!!!
Mommie.
Mommie.

MOMMIE!!!

> I'M RIGHT HERE!!!!!!

Mommie.

IT'S JUST MONEY, HONEY

Our credit card is out of control,
the stress is sucking my soul.
To be working so hard,
for money already spent
feels like eating nothing all year
to save up for Lent.
I don't know what that means,
but it's making me steam,
to know the money I make
is like a tiny DROP in a big gaping lake.

GRAMMAR

Yes, **you** want to do it.

No, **me** do it.

Yes. you.

No, **ME**, **ME**!!

You! You! You do it!

WAHHHH.

Let me explain.
When you say *you*, it's me to you.
And I am me, to me.
But I am you to you.
And you are you to me.
But you are ME to YOU
Got it?

Yes.

Okay, good.
Now here, you do it.

No, MEEEEEE!

TRAIN OF THOUGHT

IT'S
Can you cut this?
HARD
I'm thirsty.
TO
Can we go to Chuck-E-Cheese?
GET
I'm done on the potty!
A
When is Daddy coming home?
TRAIN
My belly hurts.
OF
I need paper.
THOUGHT
Can I have some chocolate milk?
IN.

EMPATHETIC EAR

Dear single sick person,
you're sick.
Boo hoo.
I feel so bad for you.
You sit alone
watching Hulu,
in a dark
quiet
room.
I'm sick too.
Just went to urgent care.
Ever tried to do that with two toddlers
yanking on your underwear?
Took a few hours
to get antibiotics.
It's a good thing my ears are clogged
so I can't hear my kids yelling
and screaming
and telling
me they want to go to the park.
"NO KIDS, THERE'S NOTHING TO DO!"
Because I'm SICK.
So we're going home,
to REST.
And by rest I mean:
doing the laundry,
and scrubbing the floors,
and prepping the dinner,
and cleaning marker off the doors.

Unclogging the wet wipes
from the toilet tube,
and making homemade Valentines
for tomorrow's school.
How many do we need?
Forty-five?
Plus some for the teachers?
Forget it.
I'll buy them from the store.
No one cares about
anything homemade anymore.
My head hurts.
I have the sweats.
No one has asked me
if I'm feeling better yet.
My cell phone rings.
"Oh, hello, again, single friend.
You just finished all the seasons
of your show?
There's nothing left in your queue?
Oooo, I feel so bad for you.
I've got to go.
I've got the sickness too.
(But I can't let it show.)

KID SICKNESS

Four weeks of coughing,
and hacking,
and bugger sucking,
and back wacking.
The teachers at your school are
little tattle tales,
"Your kid has green boogers!"
Well whoopty doo!
Why do you think I'm paying YOU?
"We don't want to get the
other kids sick, you hear?"
You mean like that one over there?
Digging his finger into an inflamed ear?
Or that one, with the crusty nose?

And what about Polly over there,
hacking and
sweating
and snozzle dripping like a hose?
I mean, really.
But you're right.
My kid DOES have green boogers.
I know, because they leaked on me
ALL NIGHT.

We'll go.

PERFECT MATH

One
Two
Three
Eleven
Twelve
Eleventeen
Eleventeen
Eleventeen.

STOP SENDING US SHIT

The presents are lovely.
You're so incredibly kind.
BUT PLEASE STOP SENDING US SHIT!
I'm loosing my mind.

I don't know what to do.
I clean out the toy bin
over and over again
only to have it re-filled
with singing stuffed rats,
and plastic toy cars,
puzzles
and lego
and stuffed toys no one will use.
STOP SENDING US SHIT!

This house is now a shit free zone.
I'll give you money to keep it AWAY.
Just keep it, okay?
Fine.
Yes.
Go ahead.
Mail the package.

The shit free rule starts tomorrow, instead.

DIET

I have a highly demanding job,
it's stressful
and hard
and I'm underpaid...
so I eat
chocolate
and peanuts
and broken up snap peas
to make it through my day.
I eat
tortilla chips,
apple slices,
coffee,
goldfish,
pink jellybeans,
congealed pasta noodles,
stale crackerjacks,
baked cheetos,
nachos,
and authentic spicy LA tacos.
(Then I blow my nose.)
Then I suck on candy that disolves nice and slow.
Wait, it's six o'clock.
Dinner time...I'd better go!

EXERCISE

There's a new form of Yoga!
You really should try it.
You just need a mat and a child.
(No need to diet!)
Spread the mat on the floor,
arch your back,
and push your palms down.
Now take a deep breath
and let your child climb on your head.
Enjoy the sensation
as they pull on your hair.
Just breathe through the pain.
Now go up to cobra and
then forward to into plank.
Let your little one ride you
like you're a pony named "Hank."
Keep it there!
What?
You really can't hold it?
Come on,
FEEL THE BURN!
Forget it.
Lay on the floor.
You did it
You're through.
Check that off of your things to do.

TODDLER THEOLOGY

Happy Birthday to Evie!
Are you sure she's three?
She looks like the same person to me.

I wash my armpits
so my teacher can't see me.

Are we going to die?
And then come back as a bug?
Or a donkey?
And Micheal Jackson is not coming back?
Because he was a zombie?

And if God made us
Then who made God?
Who is God's God?

A LOVE STORY

Oh, almonds,
you're so good.
I can't stop eating you.
I know I should,
but I won't.
You're the only nut for me.
I hope you last until eternity.
I'm so happy with you in the palm of my hand.
Your salty residue
and chewy body
make me want to
eat you all up.
So I do!
And now you're done.
Just dust in the bag.
You've left me
here alone.
I'll just sit here and cry.
Then pull myself together.
Kiss my hubby goodnight.
Then stretch out my belly
and go downstairs,
because I have cashews
hiding in the basement.

SELF-CONFIDENCE

It must be hard to be me,
always caring
and staring
in the mirror...
wanting to see
if everyone likes me.
But no one cares,
and codependence is sad,
emotions feel bad.
But I can't shut them off.
I can't help myself...
got to make sure everyone *else* is happy.
It is so exhausting.
So I won't do it anymore!
I've turned over a new leaf.
I'm now worry-free.
But first, let me ask...
Do you like me, for me?

JUST DO IT ALREADY

Why don't you empty the dishwasher?
It only takes a minute.
You could probably do it in even less
if you were out to win it.
It's quick and easy!
And then the dishes get out of the sink!
I just don't get why it is so HARD!
Just do it,
and then it's DONE!
What's that?
Why can't I?
I don't have time,
I've got to run!!!

THREE BUTTS

I get home from busting my hump.
And I just want to slump
on the sofa
and watch bad TV
with a salad piled high
in front of me.
But no rest for the weary.
I'm starting to get teary.
Because I'm so darn hungry.
So I make dinner
and sit there.
Three butts on one chair.
Munching on Brie.
Mindlessly.

CONVERSATIONS WITH THE BABYSITTER

Babysitter, "If you share, then it's fair."
My child, "Life's not fair."
Babysitter (shocked) "Who told you THAT?"
My child, "Mommy did."

MOTHER'S DAY TEA

The school has a Mother's Day Tea.
That's so sweet,
but why does it have to be
at seven flipin' thirty
in the MORNING?
Next year for Mother's Day Tea,
I'm sending in Dad
dressed like me.
HE can shove his face in the coffee cake
while I go to the spa
or take a trip to the lake.
(After I sleep in
and go to the gym.)
Now THAT would be a
Mother's Day treat.

GO THE F*CK TO SLEEP

I got, "Go the F*uck To Sleep"
at my baby shower.
I wanted to ask,
"Who would keep such a vile book?
It's crass
and it's rude.
What a lousy attitude."
But now that my kids are 3 and 5
they stay up late
and they like to chit-chat.
And my daughter plays with her toy cat.
And then they both have to pee.
So, I call up to them calmly,

"Hey kids, time for bed.
It's well past ten-thirty!
Not one more peep."

Then I mutter to myself,

"GO THE F*UCK TO SLEEP!!!"

86400 SECONDS

My days are filled with
cleaning up play dough
and having to scream,
"BE NICE TO YOUR SISTER!"
like a marine.
I feel useless,
and sad,
and a little mean.
As I tell my two toddlers they can't have
more ice cream.
And no. No TV!
And don't dump out the crayons.
Or put chips down the sink.
And toothpaste is NOT to drink!
I sweep the floor
a hundred times a day.
The amount that gets on it
creates much dismay.
Is that a battery under the floorboard?
And a broken screw?
And THERE'S the missing insert to my shoe.
Why does every word out of your mouths
have to be whining?
Where are your "please-es?"
What's it going to take to get through to you?
"WE USE KIND WORDS
IN THIS FAMILY."

And now you're writing, "I love you."
on my back.
How did you get so damn cute?
You smell clean and soft.
Your hair is silky smooth,
your voice is so precious,
and your tummy so soft.
I want to nibble your leg
and eat you all up.
Now let's stop messing around.
It's time for bed,
So we can get up
and do it all over again...

Index

U

V

W

To my parents, for taking me on countless creative expeditions as a child, thank you.

To my husband, for always fueling my fire of passion and excitement. You are an amazing husband & father. (Even though your nipples are useless.)

And, most of all, to my kids. You are delightful blessings, wrapped in lipstick smears and spilled nail polish. Thank you for your inspiration, hugs, and chaos. I love you to the moon.

TO FIND OUT MORE ABOUT MICHELLE LANG VISIT:
WWW.RELAXATIONBASEDLIFESTYLE.COM
OR
@THEMICHELLELANG | @RELAXATIONBASEDLIFESTYLE

For my kids, who changed the meaning of "blowout" for me. I love you despite it all.

For my hubby, who can dinner roll a baby like no one's business. And for my amazing parents who never limited my Mario Kart 64 play time but always encouraged my path in art.

To find out more about Holli's Art visit:
www.hollijacobsonart.com
or
@HolliJacobson

MORE INFORMATION

If you have a poem you would like to submit for consideration for publication in the next parenting poetry parody, please email:
Assist@RelaxationBasedLifestyle.com

WHERE THE SANITY ENDS is brought to you by RBL (pronounced "rebel"), which stands for Relaxation Based Lifestyle, a multi-faceted company founded by
Michelle Lang & Ian Nelms.

Visit www.RelaxationBasedLifestyle.com
for more information

Let's unite our socials!
@RelaxationBasedLifestyle
@TheMichelleLang

Trenton

Discover more books from
RBL PUBLISHING

A MERMAID'S GUIDE:
Empower Your Child in Water and in Life.

A Mermaid's Guide is a modern, holistic swim method focused on
turning every child into a safe, joyful swimmer.
(Starting in the bathtub.)

Written by Michelle Lang, graduate of the WSI (Water Safety
Instructor) Red Cross course and swim instructor to the stars,
A Mermaid's Guide is your new, must-have parenting book.

Get your copy today!

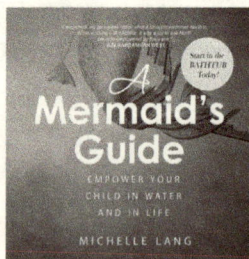

Audible, Hardcover, Paperback, Kindle

Children's books coming soon:

Under the Rug

Join Andy on a quest to discover the TRUTH about what is under the rug. Is it leeches? Cockroaches? Or something far more disgusting?

Under the Rug is entertainment sprinkled with unique vocabulary words, alluring alliteration, and energizing illustrations to help every child fall in love with reading.

Bubble's Big Adventure

A pure, peaceful bubble, named Bubble, soars through the sky to see what it can discover. Along the way, Bubble meets other bubbles who influence how Bubble looks and feels. Will Bubble stay the clear bubble it once was or become a different bubble all together?

Bubble is a story about how other people's emotions affect us and how to stay true to yourself.

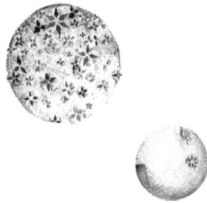

Toddy the Dot

There was once a dot named Toddy. Toddy knew a lot of other dots existed, but Toddy still felt very alone. All the other dots were part of shapes. Shapes that fit perfectly together. Every day Toddy wandered from shape to shape, hoping to find a place to fit in.

Toddy the Dot is a story about how to navigate negative emotions and make friends.

My Kids get up in
a am hour ...
But this Cold. Brew Will
give Me
My POWER

YOUR POEM

(GO AHEAD, VENT IT OUT.)

YOUR POEM
(IT HELPS, PINKI PROMISE.)

YOUR POEM
(JUST LET YOUR FEELINGS FLY.)

YOUR POEM
(No one will ever see it...)

UNLESS you want to send it to us for consideration to be included in the next book...